NLP

Through The Use Of Neuro Linguistic Programming You May Train Your Mind For Success And Learn To Influence Others

(Techniques FromNeuro Linguistic Programming That Are Straightforward For Overcoming Phobias)

FikretSchauer

TABLE OF CONTENT

Introduction 1

The Skill Of Financial Restraint And Planning 10

Indicators Of Manipulation 15

There Will Be No Starvation, Calorie Counting, Or Foods That Are Off Limits 21

How To Strengthen Your Psychic Defences And Fight Off Manipulation 27

Case Studies On More Sinister Aspects Of Psychology 36

Cavemen Lounging On The Sand 45

Sounds That Are Based On Energy Are Called Mantras. 60

The Use Of Neuro-Linguistic Programming (Nlp) Techniques To Convince Your Mind And Train Your Brain To Believe In Your Ability To Achieve Your Goals. 83

Instruments That Can Help You Get The Most Out Of Your Self-Hypnosis Sessions 92

How To Use Neuro-Linguistic Programming (Nlp) To Better Regulate Your Feelings: 102

Hypnosis 108

Utilising Nlp As A Method Of Influence 115

Then, Exactly, Can You Explain What Neuro-Linguistic Programming Is? 127

Breaks In The Loop And Interrupts In The Pattern 135

Acquiring Confidence Through The Use Of Nlp 140

Psychopaths Are Incapable Of Feeling The Suffering Of Other People In Any Way. 146

The Use Of Nlp In Business 152

The Unbounded Potential That Exists Within Each Of Us 163

Techniques Of Effective Reframing Based On Nlp 167

Introduction

Do you understand what it means to have an attitude that is productive? When you have a productive attitude, you make the most efficient use of the resources at your disposal. Your efforts, energy, and time are the resources at your disposal. It indicates that you are not attempting to accomplish everything at once or to complete tasks in the fastest manner feasible. It is making the most of the things you have while still having fun and giving your best effort. There are a few traits or attributes that will be helpful to you in achieving your goal, and they are listed below for your convenience.

These are the following:

Curiosity means that you are open to discovering new things, questioning existing ideas and notions, and actively seeking them out. You have the desire to increase the amount that you know and comprehend now.

To be Motivated or to Have Desire - If you do not have these things, there is nothing that will motivate you to become better and make development. Inertia is the state that results when a person lacks the desire to accomplish anything, and it is destructive to forward movement.

Vision is the ability to envision what you desire, which enables you to concentrate and provides you with thoughts about the kind of result you would want to see. It would be difficult to work towards your objective if you did not keep this in mind.

The capacity to evaluate a variety of circumstances in an impartial manner or to see things in their true form is an example of critical thinking. You are able to evaluate the positives and negatives of the situation and make modifications as necessary.

Self-confidence may be defined as the conviction and trust that one is entirely able to do everything that one sets their mind to. If you do not have this, you will never be able to live up to your full potential.

Perseverance is required, since the majority of things will not come easy. You have to have the mentality that will allow you to triumph over challenges. You can only accomplish what you set out to do if you push yourself and keep going no matter what. Never give in to the idea that you can't do anything because of your circumstances, the viewpoints of other people, or the roadblocks you face.

A Optimistic Viewpoint Your outlook, regardless of whether it is positive or negative, will determine your success or failure. You can do everything you put your mind to if you have a good attitude, but if you have a negative thinking, you will fail even before you get started.

Being open-minded gives you the ability to think of original and interesting new ideas. You will have an attitude that is welcoming and receptive to brand new experiences.

Maintaining a sense of equilibrium is essential if you want to carry out your daily activities successfully. It is necessary to make progress towards one's objectives, but one must also make time to relax and refresh oneself. If you put too much pressure on yourself or attempt to take on too much, you will eventually grow irritated and exhausted from all of your efforts.

You may cultivate a productive mentality and position yourself to achieve your objectives in a way that is more efficient if you make sure that you have those aspects in your life. You can also increase your mind's ability to operate better if you form positive habits and work towards that goal. You have more time available to you than you now realise. You aren't busy. The outcomes that you want can only be achieved via taking action, and your future self will be grateful to you for doing so. That is something that can be assisted with via the use of NLP.

It is astonishing how rapidly you can learn how to change your behaviours whenever you want, thus it is also wonderful how quickly you can learn how to do so. NLP may be used to break bad behaviours such as nail biting, smoking, and poor sleeping patterns. People who utilise NLP to transform their life often express scepticism about the speed at which change may take place. Things can be different after only one session. One time, a guy was able to quit a habit of biting his nails that he had had for 17 years by using a simple NLP approach that only took 25 seconds.

In a single session, some people have been able to kick behaviours that have plagued them for their whole lives. You may acquire the mental skills you need to be successful in life via the practise of NLP. When using NLP methods, one of the most important things that you do is take a step back and try to watch yourself in the way that you would want to see yourself.

When you really perform these things in a certain manner, in a very intentional way, you will be able to construct a mental picture so compelling that you attract it into your life. This may seem very basic, and you may be wondering, "What's the big deal?" but when you do this, you will be able to attract everything you want into your life. You will become a magnet, being dragged away from your old self and into your new self as the person who is no longer tied down by their old habits. In other words, you will become the person who is no longer enslaved by your previous habits.

You will develop into the kind of person you have always envisioned becoming for yourself. You will experience dissociation throughout an NLP session, during which you will see yourself in your mind in a captivating and novel manner. This is the key to NLP's effectiveness. This method has a great deal of mysticism as well as strength. Repetition, visualisation, and imaginative thinking are essential components of NLP procedures.

Because the unconscious mind is not aware of the difference between actual and imagined experiences, it is possible to train the mind to form new habits by engaging in mental rehearsal and repetition. In point of fact, many working professionals find that mental rehearsal helps them do their jobs more effectively. You don't have to physically carry out the behaviour over and over again in order to modify your habits; all you have to do is mentally rehearse them. You will learn to correlate your new behaviour with a particular trigger in a great number of the NLP approaches. This triggering event could be a sensation, or it might be an item like a telephone. When you frequently link that trigger with your new habit, you will start to establish a habitual reaction that will eventually be unleashed when the trigger is offered. This response is what you refer to as the "habitual response."

The Skill Of Financial Restraint And Planning

In the previous chapter, you were hopefully given the underlying framework for how you can start raising the numbers in your savings account. If not, you may read the previous chapter again. Increasing your revenue is, of course, merely the first step in the war; it's not even the most important one. Knowing how to save money and create a budget is a very important part of having financial intelligence and being able to organise your finances effectively. If you ask those who are knowledgeable about money and finance, you can be sure that they will tell you that the most fundamental aspect of being financially savvy is being able to create and stick to a budget. It is not sufficient to know how to bring in the money in order to succeed. It is of equal significance that you be aware of how to make use of the money that you already possess.

The skill of budgeting is going to get extensive coverage over the whole of this chapter. Think of a budget as a tool that you may use to regulate the flow of your money so that you can achieve your financial goals. You will be able to make sure that the money you have worked so hard to earn remains with you and keep track of where your dollars could be going if you have enough reserves and a well-thought-out budget plan in place. At its most fundamental level, a budget plan is a concrete reference point that specifies how much money is flowing into your life, how it is being moved about, and how it is being spent by you.

If you want to one day be financially self-sufficient and secure, it is absolutely necessary for you to make the effort to sit down, take some time, and design a sensible budget plan for yourself. You will discover how budgeting may assist put you in better situations to make sensible choices about what to do with your money if you read this chapter. These decisions will include your money. To put it simply, having a budget will assist you in avoiding being careless with the administration of your financial resources. Because you are required to pause and give careful consideration to each transaction, having a budget will drive you to adopt a more deliberate strategy on how you spend your money. You will be required to evaluate the appropriateness of each spending in light of the financial plan that you set up for yourself and impose upon yourself.

Earlier, we discussed the significance of having sound financial self-awareness and how cultivating this ability is essential to achieving high levels of financial intelligence. You will be in the greatest position to always have a clear picture of the condition of your financial situation if you create and stick to a budget. It compels you to take an honest inventory of your routines, whether they are beneficial or detrimental, so that you are constantly aware of the part that your choices play in the growth of your financial situation. In this chapter, you will learn all you need to know about creating a budget and adhering to it after it has been established. After all, the success of a budget is entirely contingent upon the manner in which its guidelines are applied to the individual's life.

On top of that, developing and sticking to a budget is going to significantly improve your ability to put money away. People are prone to falling into the trap of wanting to utilise whatever money they earn as soon as they get it much too often. They invest their money on activities, such as vacations, dinners, and entertainment, as well as material possessions, such as clothing, jewellery, and electronic devices. After accounting for all of their expenses, however, they discover that they do not have sufficient funds remaining for savings. This is a problem for them. This chapter will also provide a more in-depth examination of saving, including the reasons why it is necessary as well as the means by which adhering to a budget may assist you in accumulating money for the future.

When you look at someone who is financially savvy, you won't always find them dressed out in expensive stuff or driving flashy automobiles. They do not always take extravagant trips or participate in extravagant feasts. Without a doubt, they are able to accomplish that goal. However, the most crucial thing that individuals who are financially savvy understand is why it is essential for them to refrain from being careless with their money and the significance of conserving money.

Indicators Of Manipulation

Now comes the fun part of the modification process: getting into the meat of it! When you have mastered the ability to properly analyse another person, the next step is to master the ability to effectively influence that person! In this section, you will get an understanding of the many manipulation strategies that are available, from which you should choose one depending on what motivates your subject.

Once you know how to do it, manipulation is simple; thus, take your time and put all of your attention into really learning these methods so that you can depend on them in the future. It is very important that you do not miss any of these phases until you have really gotten the hang of analysing individuals.

The art of manipulation will not be nearly as successful for you if you have not done extensive research on the individual you are attempting to control; thus, you need to take your time and become an expert in this aspect first.

After that, achieving mastery in Manipulation will be an immeasurably more pleasant process. If you have previously done a good job of analysing your topic, you will probably discover that it only takes you a short amount of time to understand the idea and put these strategies into action. If you believe that you are prepared, continue reading for the most effective and time-tested methods of manipulation now available.

Encourage people to reject your offer.

If you want to ask someone for anything, such as a sale or something significant, you should often begin by asking them for something that you already know they would refuse. This is because you want to get a feel for how they will respond to your request. You may do this by asking the person for something absurd or ridiculous first, and then asking for what you want to ask for after that. This will encourage the individual to say no to you, which is what you want. You want to present it in such a way that it is similar to a two-part option, giving the impression that there is not a third choice.

You did not inquire as to whether or not they wanted to proceed with absolutely no warranty at all. Instead, you presented them with the option of signing a contract that was for either four or six years' duration. This is the one you should try to offer to them since the six-year warranty will only cost them an additional $100 and will provide them with protection for an additional two years. However, you must first succeed in convincing them to agree with you. They are prompted to reflect about it because of the way you have stated it here.

After that, you may say something along the lines of, "Just so you know, the additional two years will only set you back an additional one hundred dollars, and it will protect you from everything from damage to natural breakdown." Protecting your money is something that I consider to be an absolute must. By doing so, you have successfully removed the concept of "no warranty" from their consciousness and transformed the provision into a "necessity." You have also provided them with the option to purchase an extra two years of protection for the low price of $100.

They are more likely to choose with that choice since it is superior than the shorter warranty at almost the same cost. This makes it more likely that they will go with that option. It is much simpler to persuade someone to agree with what you want if you first convince them to reject what you don't want and then ask them to agree with what you do want. Some further instances are the following: - "So, will that be a five-year contract or a two-year?" - "Do you want to go on a date to the top of the Eiffel tower or the Keg tomorrow night?"

"Would you rather stay here by yourself and wait with all of these strange people around, or would you rather come with me and keep me company while I run errands?"

You have the ability to choose which of the two options the other person will reply to by manipulating the way you phrase things so that it seems as if the person only has two options, and both of those options are ones you have chosen for them. They are more likely to respond yes to the one you want them to agree with because you have purposely made one of them ridiculous or uncommon, or because it is the only one to which they would most likely not agree.

There Will Be No Starvation, Calorie Counting, Or Foods That Are Off Limits.

There are just three guidelines to follow while eating:

1. Only consume food when you feel it is necessary.

2. Chew your meal thoroughly and savour each bite as you gently consume it.

3. Cease when you feel that you have accomplished enough.

This means: 1. There will be no starvation.

2. There are no foods that are strictly prohibited.

3. Don't worry about keeping track of your calorie intake.

You do not need to be concerned about keeping track of calories. Even if you are still hungry, after you have consumed a particular number of calories, your brain quickly sends a signal to your body to urge you to stop eating. Counting calories is a path that can only end in starvation. Do you recall what happens to your body when you allow yourself to get starved? Because the body can feel when there is a deficit of food or when there is no supply at all, it will slow down the metabolism. There is no use in going on a diet for a short period of time if you are just going to end up gaining the weight back.

Keeping track of your calories may be really difficult. Do you intend to spend the rest of your life keeping track of the number of calories you eat? No one, not even those who are really skinny, ever counts calories. They do not deprive themselves of food and they do not have to be concerned about the number of calories that they consume. It's not counting calories that gives them such a trim physique; it's the good habits and lifestyle that they follow.

You are also free to consume any food you choose at any time. Since there are no prohibited meals, you are free to consume anything you choose. I had been inquiring about it with a few authorities on the topic before. And their responses were, "The reason someone becomes overweight is because they eat too much and participate in insufficient amounts of physical activity." Not as a result of regularly consuming fast food or junk food." To begin, I wasn't completely in agreement with what they said, but when I think about it, it does make sense. Even though he doesn't eat any meat, one of my friends is overweight. This is quite strange to me.

You do not have to put unnecessary stress on yourself by restricting your diet to foods that are rich in fibre, low in sugar, high in protein, and other such characteristics. If you eat just when you are hungry and stop when you are content, you should be able to continue eating all of your favourite foods while still maintaining or reducing your weight. If you are let to consume whatever foods you like, you will find that it is much simpler to feel content. If you are forced to consume foods that you do not like, you will not feel satiated after eating them and will thus overeat. You are aware that there will be another day, so you may save some of the food for the next day so that you do not overindulge.

There are no meals that you are not allowed to consume, but you should keep in mind that you do have the ability to make a decision. Why would you choose to eat at a fast food restaurant when you have the option to bring food from home with you? Why would you choose to drink a soft drink when you could be drinking juice if you had the choice? Why go with the option that is less desirable when you have a superior one? Offer yourself the chance to consume a diet that is healthy in all aspects. It would be quite helpful if you also consulted an expert nutritionist or dietitian on this matter. They are coaches for weight reduction who can be relied on and trusted.

How To Strengthen Your Psychic Defences And Fight Off Manipulation

You have most likely previously had this thought: if anybody else in my life knew these secrets, they could use them against me. After digesting the content of this chapter, you won't need to be concerned about this matter, despite the fact that the concept itself may be somewhat unsettling. Using a technique known as psychic resistance, we will instruct you on how to construct sturdy mental barriers; but, mastering this skill will need some time and effort on your part. In Chapter 4, I will provide you with several helpful hints to assist you in protecting yourself from being manipulated.

The exercise we covered in the first chapter will be the most helpful practise you can get for protecting yourself from the manipulation of another person. You probably remember that one of your assignments was to write a page or two describing your perspective on various matters.

You will benefit from this activity since it will help you strengthen the concepts you already have about a subject. If you have a lot of words to back up your views, it will be much more difficult for a manipulator to dominate your mind or influence you if you have a lot of words. When a person does not develop or expand on their thoughts, they are particularly vulnerable to NLP since all the manipulator needs to do is offer them new ideas, ideas that seem to be more thought out than the person's original ideas. This makes the person very easy to manipulate.

People who haven't given a topic a lot of consideration have a greater propensity to fall into the manipulator's trap and embrace their concept. This is because theories that have more support look more plausible to people who haven't given a topic a lot of thought. In the event that they are subjected to manipulation, they will accept the concept that prompts a change in their behaviour.

You will continue to do the same exercise, but with certain modifications, if you want to alter the structure of your mind so that anything like this can never happen to you again. You are going to want to create this following piece of writing on a fresh question so that you may demonstrate flexibility. In this section, please explain your stance on the use of animals in research by writing a page or two.

This time around, one thing that will be new for you is that you will need to be ready for the opposing viewpoint of the debate. If you aren't prepared for the manipulator's counterpoints, they may be able to convince you to take their side of the argument. The paper may begin on the positive grounds of your argument; nevertheless, in order to create strong mental resistance, you will want to devote the majority of the write-up on rebuttals to the manipulator's counter-arguments.

Obviously, we are just doing this for practise. It is quite unlikely that your stance on the use of animals in experiments is the thing you want to be defended against the most. We do this because when you write down whatever your stance is, you get a much clearer and more complete picture of that position. It gets you ready for the many different kinds of arguments that might be made against you.

You should do the same exercise no matter what the situation is. Write about the concepts that are the most significant to you, and explain in your own words the reasons why you hold the viewpoints that you do. If you prepare in this manner, the first person who challenges your views will be taken aback by the seeming impregnability of your positions. Because you may do this exercise with a wide variety of different items, and because we don't know what aspects of your life are most important to you, we can't advise you which positions to use for it. Just keep in mind that putting your thoughts down on paper not only solidifies and validates all of the concepts of the world that you have, but that doing so is also the most effective technique to create mental resistance against manipulators.

You may have anticipated that if you keep doing this exercise on a regular basis, it will not only help you protect yourself against other manipulators, but it will also make you a better psychological manipulator in general. Writing down your ideas and thoughts might help you feel more certain about them. People will assume that you are talking the truth if you exude confidence. When other people who are attempting to manipulate you see how steadfast you are in your views, they will eventually give up trying to do so.

The unfortunate reality is that there are NLP practitioners in the world who take use of these psychological practises in order to do harm to other individuals. You, on the other hand, are well-equipped to remain unaffected by the strategies that they are employing since you are familiar with both the techniques that they are using and the theoretical underpinning that they are utilising.

However, this does not imply that things are simple all of the time. The fact that we are not always conscious when we are being influenced is the primary factor that contributes to the difficulty of the situation. After all, we are constantly being targeted by other individuals and businesses that are employing neurolinguistic programming (NLP) against us without even being aware of it. In the next chapter, we will go more deeply into the subject of NLP as it occurs in the background of our day-to-day lives. Because manipulation is nothing more than influencing someone's thinking about things, which is not always a negative thing to do, there is nothing intrinsically wrong with this as long as it does not negatively affect us.

Nevertheless, when these individuals and organisations are using it to damage us, it is imperative for us to recognise that they are doing so. The good news is that we are going to discuss the indications that you may look out for to determine whether or not a manipulator is utilising NLP and psychology to control your mind, read your thoughts, or manipulate you in some other way.

You must to be ready to consider the situation from the prospective of the possible manipulator before delving into the particular warning indicators. You are familiar with what it is like to be on the receiving end of a scenario for yourself, and as a result, you may be able to determine whether you are being influenced if you choose to carry out this activity by yourself. Being able to perceive things from the perspective of another person is another vital talent for someone who uses psychological manipulation. The more you polish this skill, the simpler it will be to grow your mental resistance.

Because of its ability to keep us from slipping into a certain trap, this ability is very crucial. You see, there is a pitfall in making the assumption that we are aware of the appearance of a manipulator. You should be aware that manipulating others through NLP and psychology is possible for absolutely everyone on the face of the earth, regardless of whether or not you believe you resemble the kind of person that generally manipulates others. You can't depend on generalisations to tell you whether or not you're being controlled, since they're not accurate enough.

When we depend on stereotypes to determine whether or not we are being manipulated, we are doing it in a way that causes us to grossly underestimate the significance of psychological resistance. Because of this, we are susceptible to being influenced and having our minds affected without even being aware of the fact. You can't allow the fact that you believe a manipulator has a noisy personality, a charming personality, a quiet personality, or any other quality colour your picture of the scenario in any way.

Case Studies On More Sinister Aspects Of Psychology

It is possible that Stalin was one of the most ruthless and lethal dictators in the history of the world. In spite of the fact that he was known for using a ruthless and terrifying leadership style, he did use certain elements of persuasion in his strategies. Stalin, in contrast to previous dictators who began their reign by the use of brutal force, such as Idi Amin of Uganda, first went out to the populace by telling them warped versions of the truth in an effort to persuade a subset of the general population to support his goals.

The people of the Soviet Union were left in a state of crippling anxiety as a result of Joseph Stalin's reign of terror. His method of mind control was almost unmatched by that of any other political figure. His foot troops obeyed his instructions without question and were given the authority to murder, maim, and punish anybody at their discretion, regardless of whether or not the victim had committed any crime.

Because there were no laws in place, the residents were never sure when they may be found guilty of breaking one of the laws. For any cause, a sentence to one of the GULAG (forced labour camps) might be handed down to anyone. There was a remote possibility that I might survive my time in the GULAG. Even those individuals who did not have the misfortune of being committed to the GULAG for an indeterminate period of time did not discover that living in society was a secure option. People were starving to death, being murdered, or being mistreated by the guys working for Stalin, and they were dying in droves.

How did the Soviet Union sink to the point that it is unable to even exist? What strategies were put into play? Simply rhetoric! The Soviet Union really wanted there to be a change in the leadership. The people of the Soviet

Union desired greater leadership than that which was provided by Vladimir Lenin, who served as the leader of the Soviet government from 1917 and 1922. Stalin saw the opportunity and turned to the more sinister side of emotional intelligence in order to further his position in the hearts of the people.

The masses, especially the residents of the working class, were easily swayed by his persuasive speeches. They envisioned a future brimming with exciting opportunities and promising prospects. But the events that unfolded after that were nothing like what the people had hoped for. Stalin was able to easily influence the people because he understood how to take obvious concerns that would attract support from the people and mix it with well-timed emotionally-laden remarks that would trigger the proper sort of emotional reactions. This allowed Stalin to control the people in a manner that was easy for him.

Despite the fact that Stalin eventually abandoned his use of emotional control in favour of a more direct form of tyranny, he was a master of the technique.

Adolf Hitler was the sort of speaker that talked from the heart, and he was the political leader of Germany at the time. Adolf Hitler. He was well aware that basing his decisions on logic would restrict him to a very limited segment of the population. People were moved to a state of wonder as a direct result of the authenticity with which he delivered his words.

Hitler was a master of the art of persuasion, which he utilised to his disadvantage in order to manipulate a whole people into giving up their capacity to think critically. They just shifted their viewpoint and began acting without analysing the reasons why Hitler did what he did.

Hitler devoted a significant amount of time and energy to researching the strength of human emotions and the ways in which body language may be exploited to induce a desired emotional reaction. He would hone a variety of hand gestures, facial expressions, and other body motions by practising them and analysing them. He communicated his ideas to people's hearts by relying only on the power of body language, therefore avoiding the need for the human intellect to engage in logical thought. He exerted a great deal of effort towards the cultivation and improvement of this talent. There is no room for debate on the reality that he accomplished his goal.

When he eventually started to use his abilities, he would talk with such a great deal of passion that it looked as if his voice was rising from the depths of his body and into the soul of those who were listening to him. Even the slothful and unmotivated were roused by his words. He had the ability to convince even the most fearful and scepticalindividuals that his views and ideologies were correct.

Hitler did not come from a wealthy or politically significant family. His hatred for Jewish people and the anguish he felt over his country's recent humiliation both played a role in his climb to power, which he accomplished by sheer force of will and single-minded resolve.

Hitler, who was feeling depressed about the way things were going in his nation, came to the conclusion that the best way forward would be to gather an army of people under his control using various methods of mind control in order to destroy his adversaries and get his country back on its feet again.

Because Hitler was so skilled in the art of persuasion, it was not difficult for him to convince his supporters to murder other people for the "crime" of belonging to a different race and religion. But as if that were not awful enough, the individuals who carried out his sinister goal never had the impression that they were engaging in illegal activity. This was the power of persuasion that Hitler exerted over his followers; he convinced his people that the activities they were doing were morally justifiable.

War without reason was the direct outcome of all of the brainwashing and propaganda that Hitler spread via the Nazi schools. More than 40 million people lost their lives as a direct result of both the Holocaust and World War II.

It was Charles Manson.

Charles Manson is not a politician and does not hold a position of authority in any government. As a law-abiding citizen of the United States, he was entitled, as with every other citizen, to the freedoms of association and belief. Manson, on the other hand, used his freedom to associate with others to a completely different degree. About one hundred of his followers were so committed to him that they thought he was God and Satan at the same time. They were part of his following.

However, he did not achieve prominence by having his followers think that he was both God and Satan in order to garner their devotion. As a result of his ability to corrupt his followers into committing horrific atrocities, he gained a notorious reputation. They carried out his instructions without raising any objections.

Because he was able to convince his people using two powerful tools—sex and religion—Manson was able to exert a great deal of influence over the minds of his followers. When these instruments were combined with his skill at using rhetoric, he gave his followers the impression that he was nearly godlike.

He persuaded naive individuals that they could feel good from anything, and it didn't matter if it was sex, drugs, or any other methods. He was successful in doing this. Manson was able to take advantage of people's vulnerabilities by actively seeking out those who were looking for meaning and purpose in their life. As a result, he was successful in getting people to believe his bizarre songs and predictions. He saw himself as a guide and a guru, and he positioned himself in such a way as to be in the ideal position to convince his followers to buy into his views hook, line, and sinker.

Even while Manson may not have been as skilled as Stalin and Hitler in the art of persuasion, he was nonetheless able to amass a sufficient number of followers to carry out his dishonest deeds. To emphasise how manipulative Charles Manson was, he never participated in any of the killings that were done in his name. He was content to manipulate other people into doing his work for him. This demonstrates how powerful his grasp was on the thoughts of those who followed him. Mason's most notable accomplishment was getting his so-called "family" to participate in a series of murders.

Cavemen Lounging On The Sand

The guy gazed admiringly at the attractive form of the young lady as she stood on the beach in Italy without her top on. After a time, she reached for a T-shirt, pulled it over her head, and covered her breasts with it. She stooped to reach the bottom of her backpack in order to get a bottle of water. He found himself trying to get a glimpse of her chest, which was now largely obscured. He was able to get a glimpse of one of her nipples. Even though her breasts had been exposed in their entirety only a few seconds ago, he found the fleeting look that he got at them to be immensely gratifying.

Why was this more appealing than seeing her while she was in her natural state with nothing covering her? Is it possible that he stumbled onto something that he was not meant to view since it had become confidential?

Was it because he had violated a taboo by staring at something that wasn't supposed to be seen?

Was this the ultimate explanation for life's meaning? Are we, for our own pleasure and enjoyment, interested in discovering what is veiled and hidden from view? Taking from the cosmos something which does not rightfully belong to us to take? having the ability to avoid consequences while having broken the rules? Are you looking for a glimpse of the vast mysteries that underlie our existence? Are you dying to turn the page and find out who committed the crime and why?

It's possible that everybody's just naturally nosy or, at the very least, interested in other people's business. It's possible that, rather than passion, what has kept us going for the tens of thousands of years that we've been around is our natural curiosity. This soft-bodied monster, which lacks claws, teeth, and scaly armour, has been able to conquer every living creature in the earth, even fish and birds.

It would seem that civilization is nothing more than a superficial covering for men's underlying primitive tendencies. If you scratch that surface, you'll uncover our true essence lying just underneath it.

Our most basic instincts are to be kind, calm, and compassionate towards one another. The so-called "civilization" is responsible for the development of the features that are in no way animal in nature.

We presume that we have culture simply due to the fact that a significant portion of humanity are literate. Next, we make the assumption that culture is a mark of civilised society. The Black Death was immediately followed by one of the most turbulent eras in the history of Europe, which is known as the Renaissance. On the other hand, as a result of it, magnificent works of art were produced in Italy and France, which is one of the indicators of what we now refer to as civilization.

The guy found himself in the centre of a large group of archaic locals when he arrived at that beach. The children enjoyed themselves while their parents took it easy. On the beach, ladies without bras strolled about or reclined in various positions. Men dressed just in loincloths marched, slept, and swam throughout this time. Canoes were being paddled in a laid-back fashion as they made their way out to sea.

Even though it had a wild appearance, this location was really secure. People were lounging about here in almost their natural state. The sentiment may be summed up by the overused term "paradise," which was printed on a beach towel. Two weeks out of every fifty-two, we are able to reconnect with our authentic, primal selves. We are considered to be "civilised" throughout the remaining ninety-six percent of the time.

The guy and his wife complied with the dress requirement by changing into their swimsuits while discretely hiding behind towels that were wrapped over their emaciated bodies. "Are you going to remove your top?" He inquired.

Why did he encourage his wife to exhibit her breasts to those who did not know them? When they were living their normal lives back in their hometown, he would have attacked a Peeping Tom if he had seen him looking through the bedroom window from a mile away. However, in this case, those things, which every man fully has, were able to be exposed to a thousand unidentified bags of testosterone with the complete cooperation of the guy who is envious.

While he was attempting to remove the sand from his hands, he reflected on the fact that the sand likely included bits of human skin as a result of the natural exfoliation process caused by the hundreds of people that visited the beach over the season. A plethora of ailments, including athlete's foot, psoriasis, warts, and a whole host of others, were lounging around on his towel and all over his body!

The absence of wind left wind surfers stranded on the water. They were all standing on their boards as if in a queue for something, and they all gave off the impression that they were irritated by the fact that nature had a sense of comedy.

After a sufficient amount of wind had carried them beyond the point where they could safely swim back, the wind died down, leaving them in the doldrums.

The scene brought to mind those nature films in which indigenous people stand in boats and spear fish with spearguns.

As he made himself comfortable on his towel, his thoughts wandered to a time fifty thousand years in the past, when man was an emerging power rather than a dominant one, and how the world may have been different. There was a shift in the equilibrium. The efforts of mankind, much like a sand castle, would be destroyed and carried away by the might of nature.

Even at the present time, the four constituents of the universe have the ability to predominate. The fire of volcanoes, the water in tidal waves and floods, the earth when it is split by earthquakes, and the amazing bursts of energy that may be found in hurricanes and tornadoes are all examples of natural disasters.

Concrete and steel are treated with the same lack of concern by these natural occurrences when they take place as a sandcastle does when waves are present. Important examples include the tsunami that struck Indonesia, the destruction that took place in New

Orleans, and the earthquakes that occurred in Pakistan.

After that, the leaders of the church began to question whether or not God existed since he had not stopped them. despite the fact that they had been percolating for many years. notwithstanding the cynical labelling of these occurrences by insurers as "acts of God."

However, it was precisely those things that were responsible for the formation of seas and mountains millions of years ago. They were and still are the people that put forth the most effort to construct our world.

His brain was processing information at a breakneck speed. People from the United States, Germany, Italy, and England were seen peacefully coexisting on a beach that just a few decades before they would have violently contested ownership over.

People were able to rest under the same sun since they were no longer concerned with competing nations or doctrine. For thousands of years, the authority of politicians and churchmen had caused division among the population.

This inclination to trust and relax on the beach is an illustration of the primitive innocence that exists inside us when we are not in danger.

Who is making the threat? When arranged in a hierarchy, it would seem that the answer is all of the people. the upper echelons of organisations, governments, countries, and religious institutions.

They were all relieved to finally be away from their jobs, nations, politicians, and other public officials for a little time. Here they were. It's possible that they were able to relax despite their precarious position since there was no power basis.

Pyramids of power are rather common in the natural world. The alpha males and females of each pack exercise dominance over the members of their pack that are lower in rank. Any gathering of individuals working for any company is governed by Episcopalian principles in addition to more sophisticated corporate ladders and political corridors of influence. The power that can be mustered by a nation's armed forces and weapons does the same objective.

We are not more civilised than our forefathers despite the fact that we have pinstripes, bishops' robes, and atomic weapons. They were able to wield their muscles, clubs, and stones, but this was more for the sake of sex and food than total authority. Gorillas are known for their civilised but aggressive demeanour. It is better to threaten than to really create carnage. After an extremely violent and terrible beginning, humanity eventually pulled itself together and gave birth to civilization.

The pair found a comfortable spot, used the umbrellas to create the core of their pitch, and then used towels to both extend and guard the territory they had created. This belonged to them. Their scattered remains served as a warning to others, just as effectively as the urination pattern of a wolf would.

The ability to kick back, relax, and socialise with one's peers was a perk of the hunter-gatherer lifestyle in bygone eras. This was possible after the prey had been successfully brought down. The act of hunting and gathering now takes just a few minutes in the supermarket, which frees up more time for us to work for the benefit of others and increase their wealth.

Because of this, there is never enough time for us to sit down and relax while catching up with friends and family, unless we are on vacation and wearing loincloths.

Sounds That Are Based On Energy Are Called Mantras.

Any word that is said causes a real vibration in the physical world. If we are aware of the impact that the vibration has, then maybe over the course of time the word will come to have a meaning that is related with the effect of pronouncing that particular vibration or phrase. One level of the energy foundation for words is shown here.

Intention is still another layer. When the real physical vibration is combined with the mental intention, the vibration will then carry an extra mental component that will impact the effect of expressing it. Sound is the carrier wave, and intention is superimposed over the wave form in the same way as a coloured gel affects the look and impact of white light.

In either use, the term refers to anything having to do with energy. This concept is nowhere more applicable than it is with regard to Sanskrit mantras. The only definition that will stand the test of time is the outcome or impact that comes from repeating the mantra. Mantras are connected with a broad meaning, but this connotation isn't what defines them.

Mantras cause waves of thought-energy to be produced.

The human consciousness may be thought of as a collection of many states of awareness that are dispersed throughout the body, both the subtle and the physical levels. Each organ has a rudimentary awareness of its own, which enables it to carry out the activities that are unique to that organ. Then there are the many different systems. A number of the body's systems, including the cardiovascular system, the reproductive system, and others, each include a number of organs or other portions of the body that operate at somewhat different phases of the same process. In addition to the organs, each system is also connected with its own distinct kind of primal awareness. All of these take place inside of the physical body. Within the subtle body, functions and states of awareness that are analogous to those found outside of it also exist. Therefore, individual organ awareness is superimposed by system consciousness, which in turn is superimposed once more by subtle body equivalents and consciousness, and so on and so forth ad infinitum.

The ego, with its self-defined 'I'-ness, acquires a prominent status among the delicate noise of random, unconscious ideas which pulse through our bodies. Naturally, our body is able to 'pick up' the vibrations that are being produced by other species in the area. The end effect of this is that the unconscious mind is always being subjected to a plethora of vibrations that are passing through and inside it. A tremendous vibration is initiated by mantras, and this vibration correlates to a certain frequency of spiritual energy as well as a state of awareness in its embryonic form. After some period of time, the mantra process starts to take precedence over all of the other, less significant vibrations, which finally get absorbed by the mantra. when a period of time that is unique to each person, the tremendous wave of the mantra will quiet all other vibrations. This will happen when a certain amount of time has passed. In the end, the mantra creates a condition in which the organism vibrates at a pace that is entirely in sync with the energy and spiritual state that is represented by the mantra and that is contained inside it.

A transition from one state to another takes place in the organism at this moment. The creature undergoes a minuscule transformation. In the same way that a laser is light that is coherent in a new manner, the person who becomes one with the state created by the mantra is likewise coherent in a way that did not exist previous to the conscious undertaking of repetition of the mantra. This is because the state of the person who becomes one with the state generated by the mantra is produced by the mantra.

Current method of resolution

After you have gained an understanding of the demands of the consumer, you are now prepared to provide your solution and move closer to the phases of completing the sale.

It's possible that the client will need you to really offer your solution to them in the form of a presentation that you give to a panel of decision-makers. You will discover a lot of material that will enable you to accomplish this properly in the chapter titled "Presenting Impact." This information will include some suggestions that will help you overcome any objections that are presented when you are giving your presentation. For the time being, we may limit ourselves to giving a straightforward presentation, which consists of simply you and the client having a casual conversation.

Specifying an Expected Outcome

When I was working in the telecommunications business, one of my responsibilities was to act as a technical expert during sales meetings with other salespeople. Before the start of every meeting, I would inquire, "What is our goal?" The typical response from the salesman was to look at me blankly for a few moments before saying, "Well, we'll just see what's going on, get to know them, you know."

This doesn't really do anything, does it? You'll know their response as having been phrased not as a result but as an action when you hear it. It's not the best situation, but you can't really hold it against them since, most of the time, their performance was evaluated based on their activity rather than their results. How many leads they pursued, how many meetings they attended, and so on are all examples of this. As long as they kept themselves occupied, their bosses had a tendency to ignore the fact that they were falling short of their sales quotas.

If you attend a sales meeting with the intention of having a conversation and finding out what's going on, then you can expect just that to take place. After the conclusion of the meeting, the client will most likely feel confused and upset, wondering why they wasted an hour of their time but did not make any headway in resolving the issue that they were facing with their company.

Create an opening statement by using the concepts of Well-Formed Outcomes, and then express it as if you were looking back from the conclusion of the meeting. For instance, you might say something like, "By the end of this meeting, I would like us to have made a decision on what the final solution will look like."

When you do this, the client is aware of precisely what they need to pay attention to, which enables them to feel more at ease and provides them with information of a higher quality upon which they may make their choice.

In what ways does this illustration use the concepts presented in Well-Formed Outcomes?

A good sign

It is expressed as what it is that you want to accomplish.

The phrase "I would like us to" shows that you recognise the fact that the other persons involved have a voice in this matter even if it is "under your control."

"what the final solution will look like" in its most literal form. provides a description of the result in a graphic format

The phrase "us to have made a decision" in an ecological context suggests a process that is owned jointly and invites people to declare what they want as well.

Readers with keen eyes will see the one area in which this sort of result is lacking, and that is the fact that it is not genuinely within your control. This is a problem that arises often in any endeavour that also involves other people since the only way to accomplish what you desire is with the agreement or cooperation of those other individuals.

Take a few minutes to read chapter 9 in the appendix right now to get an idea of how various individuals deal with the challenge that the majority of the time in life we have to depend on the assistance of other people.

Examining the level of consensus

The quickest and easiest approach to determine whether or not a client is in agreement is to just ask them and pay attention to whether or not they respond with "yes" or "no."

Do you agree that tag questions are quite helpful in this context?

"So this is the kind of thing you have in mind, right?"

If you are feeling daring, you may switch the verb tense in the tag question for a very dramatic impact. For example, you might say, "This is what you have in mind, wasn't it?"

You are able to employ the ecological check that is provided by Well Formed Outcomes whenever you use questions of this kind. In other words, keep a close eye on the consumer and pay attention to whether or not they concur.

Comments, Queries, and Concerns

A great number of approaches to dealing with objections begin with the assumption that the issue exists in the first place. In order for an objection to have any validity, the consumer must...

Has entertained the idea of purchasing the product Has considered an obstacle that would prevent them from utilising the product Is interested enough in the topic to tell you about it

Therefore, one might consider an objection to be a purchase signal, or at the very least, a hint that the consumer has shifted into "buying mode," assuming that objection is made in good faith. If I'm looking to buy a vehicle for my kid and I want to make sure the stroller will fit in the trunk, then I must have pretended to put the pushchair in the trunk. If I'm attempting to put a pushchair in the trunk, then I must have purchased the car at some time in the past.

Customers may voice complaints for a variety of reasons besides to express their dissatisfaction with the product or service. Before deciding whether or not to answer to an objection, it is usually a good idea to take a step back, allow yourself some time to think about what the issue is, and then decide.

You'll find that once you begin to explain a query or objection, if it isn't built on a strong basis, it will dissipate on its own without your further intervention. This is a common occurrence. In order to do this, you may make use of Meta Model questions.

Production of Images

I have no doubt that you are ready to understand the secret to transforming the images in your mind and embracing the transformation that will occur in your life. Now, let's get this trip started!

Imagine that you are on a tour through your mind and that you have arrived to a facility that is simply referred to as "Picture Works." It is a massive factory that has a large screen that has the capability of being painted. There are speakers for the ambient music, as well as a handbook with controls for adjusting the colours, brightness, and clarity, as well as the feelings that are linked with them. One idea at a time is entering that factory, and together they are creating a very detailed image on that screen. As soon as the painting is completed, it is immediately sent to the mind's subconscious. After that, the subconscious mind will make an identical copy of it in the shape of the activities that you will do. This is pretty much how your ideas lead to your imagination and the way you speak to yourself, which then gets imprinted into your subconscious mind and reflected in your behaviours later on.

Your thoughts directly influence the way in which your mind functions. When you reflect on an image in your mind that has been created by your thoughts, you begin to engage in internal dialogue with yourself. If the image that came into your mind was a positive one, then your thoughts and the way you talk to yourself in the future will be positive as well. On the other hand, if the image was a negative one, then your thoughts and the way you talk to yourself in the future will be negative. Your future thoughts and the way you talk to yourself in the future are dependent on the kind of picture that came into your mind. These ideas and conversations with yourself eventually manifest as feelings and emotions, which in turn direct your behaviours. Your bad conversations with yourself will lead to negative thinking, and then you will end up doing something that you shouldn't have done or that you should have known better than to do. In most cases, we fail to recognise this occurrence, and as a result, we are simply left with a great deal of regret in the future. Is it not so?

Let me share with you an encounter I had with a golfer that you will find to be related and will help you comprehend this topic better. After a poor showing on the first day of the competition the day before, an upset golfer came up to me during a call on the second day of a golf tournament to express his concern about his play on the previous day. The following is how the discussion continued after I had listened to what he had to say:

If you pay great attention to the dialogue that was just described, you'll see that the reason the golfer was having such bad thoughts was because he was thinking about how he had played the day before. His anxiety was being played out in his head like a movie, and it was also being stored in the more primitive part of his mind. Because the image he conjured up in his head was unfavourable, he found himself naturally resorting to critical internal monologue. If he maintained his level of anxiety, he would have no choice but to keep repeating to himself, "Don't miss the shot." You really must have it in order to improve your score. Just make sure you don't flub the shot. What do you believe is going to take place after this? He won't make the shot at all. If you recall me stating it to you previously, our subconscious mind does not comprehend the phrase "don't." As a result, his instruction of "Don't miss the shot" will transform into "miss the shot" for our mind. If you remember what I said, "Don't miss the shot" will turn into "miss the shot" for our mind.

You have to come to the realisation that everything you think, imagine, and say to yourself matters a great deal since it has such a significant bearing on the course of your life. Your feelings, your ideas, and even the things you do may all be influenced by the image you create in your head. You will learn how to transform these negative pictures in the coming chapters so that your internal dialogues (self-talks) change, followed by a change in your sentiments, and finally a change in your behaviours that are in harmony with them. Your life will be filled with nothing but good things if you let out positive vibes while you are feeling good and thinking clearly since those are the conditions under which you will attract them.

There are a lot of individuals in the world that are now going through tough times financially. When people think about their financial issues, the images that appear in their heads are those of going bankrupt, not having enough money to pay their bills, the amount of their loan, the amount of their credit card debt, the amount of their rent, and so on. How can a person possibly think positively when they are constantly seeing such depressing scenes in their mind? During moments like these, the poisonous ideas that go through a person's head include things like, "I am incapable of doing anything," "my life is only filled with struggles," "I am broke and I don't think I can ever earn enough," and "I can't live like this anymore." I want to expire soon. I despise my existence. These bad conversations give birth to negative sentiments, which in turn leave you feeling depressed and exhausted. You are making yourself vulnerable if you do this, and the choices you make while you are vulnerable almost always lead to unfavourable outcomes for you. My advise to all of you is to never make a choice while you are feeling as helpless as you are right now.

You may be asking how you may break out of this never-ending cycle of negativity that is destroying your life. In order to do so, you need to understand how to shift the pictures that are floating about in your head. In the following chapters, I will walk you through each stage of this procedure in sequential order. For the time being, I will bring this chapter to a close by giving you a task to do and providing some food for thought.

The Use Of Neuro-Linguistic Programming (Nlp) Techniques To Convince Your Mind And Train Your Brain To Believe In Your Ability To Achieve Your Goals.

-

Neuro-Linguistic Programming, sometimes known as NLP, is an approach that investigates how one thinks and feels. It investigates the inner language that you often use to reflect the events and experiences of your life. The study of human interaction and accomplishment, as well as the use of this information to assist individuals in reaching their full potential in all facets of life, is the focus of this field.

The ideas that underpin NLP approaches are predicated on the premise that you already possess all of the internal resources and talents required to effectually transform not just your own life but also the lives of the individuals in your immediate environment.

The use of NLP may assist you in establishing goals for yourself and taking the steps required to achieve those goals.

Simple NLP Methods that Can Assist You in Achieving Your Objectives

It's important to be explicit about the things you desire. This reaffirms the advice that has been given to you time and time again: you need to have a crystal-clear grasp of precisely what it is that you desire. You need to have a distinct mental picture of the end goal in front of you at all times. Consider it from this perspective: picture yourself on a boat out in the middle of the ocean. You will not be successful if you do not have a distinct plan for where you want to end up and instead choose to just go with the current and see where it takes you. If you walk through life without any direction or plan, how can you expect to get at the destination you desire?

Ask yourself what it is that you really want. Asking yourself things like, "If I keep doing the things I'm doing now, where will I be a year from now?" is something that is recommended by NLP. Am I content with the path that I am now on and where it will take me? What should I do differently if I find that I am not happy? What exactly would bring a smile on my face? It will be much simpler for you to determine what it is that you desire if you have answers to inquiries of a similar kind.

Develop concrete mental representations of what you want to achieve. As soon as you have determined what it is that you want to accomplish, write those goals down on paper. Consequently, if you want to purchase the home of your dreams, you should see it in your head first, down to the tiniest aspects, such as the architecture, the location, and the community. It is essential that you conjure up potent mental pictures and keep replaying them in your head over and over again. Think about the actual colours, what you see around you, the scent of the flowers, or the sound of your neighbor's dog barking in the background. This will help you be more realistic. Conjure up a mental "movie" and watch it. See what you are truly wearing on the day that you are eventually purchasing the property. Go as far as seeing what you are actually wearing on that specific day. Create a film that is as realistic and detailed as possible, as if it were truly taking place. The use of visualisation methods has reached a new plateau as a result of this.

Focus on achieving your objectives while writing them down as if you've already accomplished them. If you discover that using terms in the present tense helps, then you may go on to imagining what those words look like. Visualising the accomplishment of your objective as if it were already taking place at this very second can help you make a more significant impression. Remember that NLP teaches you and gives you the ability to go towards the things that you concentrate on carefully, so keep that in mind. You are putting yourself in a position to be successful by doing so. Using this method, you will be able to exert some control on the outcomes of certain events. It is very necessary for you to keep your attention fixed on a crystal clear and upbeat mental picture of what it is that you want to accomplish, which in this instance is purchasing your ideal home. You need to ensure that you keep your attention fixed on the target throughout the whole of the process of working towards its achievement.

Make the achievement of your objective the driving force behind your continued progress in that direction. Consider the steps you may take that will get you closer to achieving your objective. Develop some strategies for how you can continue to make progress in the situation. Imagine that you have already crossed the "finish line" and are looking back on the steps that got you there. What did you do to get there? Visualising a physical mind that has a number of key aspects could be of use to you. You will not be able to achieve the success that you want until you follow this course of action. There is a possibility that you may face challenges, but if you keep your attention fixed on the destination, you will be able to devise strategies to surmount those challenges and on with your trip. It is much easier to accomplish anything when you have a clear idea of the steps that need to be taken in order to make it a reality.

Find someone you can look up to. Try to find someone you can model yourself after and get wisdom from. Read about their achievements in the past. You can get advice from them, or if you can't get in touch with them, you may look for materials that talk about them. The biographies of most renowned and successful individuals provide advice and suggestions that readers might follow to achieve similar levels of achievement. Learn more about them by reading books and watching related videos. Educate yourself with their experiences, both positive and negative.

Act! Even if you have planned out what you want to do and know what you want to accomplish, if you don't start taking action, you won't ever accomplish anything. You must take action in order to accomplish what you set out to do since neither anything nor anyone else can do it for you. This is the first step that you must do. Take action to get the ball rolling on the path to seeing your objectives through to completion. If you want to purchase a home, you should get started saving money right away or think about finding new sources of income. One simple action is all that's required to start you moving in the right direction.

Plan! After you have started working towards your goal, the next step is to make sure that you have a detailed strategy for how you are going to accomplish it. You really need to have a timetable. Maintaining your concentration and forming constructive mental pictures of the accomplishment of your objective will help you get closer to achieving it as you go forward.

Put off a positive vibe. Having confidence does not guarantee that you will not make a mistake. It signifies that despite the fact that you could face problems, you still have the confidence to continue moving ahead. You could make a mistake, but if you take it in stride and see it as a teaching moment, you'll be able to get back on track quickly.

Keep an open mind. Even if you put a lot of effort into something, it may not pan out the way you had hoped. You are going to have to keep going and look into other possibilities.

Continue on your way. It is possible that along the path, you may experience failure, and it is also possible that you will confront rejection; nonetheless, this should not deter you from continuing to pursue your objectives. Proceed onward without stopping.

Instruments That Can Help You Get The Most Out Of Your Self-Hypnosis Sessions

Let's take a look at some of the wonderful ways in which we can actually tug at the reins of that magic we have just studied, and make it all the more effective than we might have erstwhile imagined it would be. Now that we have seen all of the wonderful techniques that are involved in the process of self-hypnosis, let's take a look at some of the wonderful ways in which the process of self-hypnosis actually involves.

Suggestions to help you get the most out of your own self-hypnosis experience

The purpose of this article is to provide you with a few pointers that will assist you in getting the most out of the process of self-hypnosis.

- Create an image in your mind of the sensation you want to experience. We have established that it is necessary for us to make use of all of our senses in order to have a clear mental image of the things that we want to do in our life. In this regard, it is essential that we make a concerted effort to concentrate on the sensation that we imagine we will have when we finally arrive at our destination. Imagine that your goal is to get a major motion picture produced. Imagine that you are standing at the premiere of the film and taking in all the adoration that is being showered upon you. Actually have all of the happy feelings that you wish you could have at that very time.

- Ensure that you are consistent, and after you've established that, expand on it. "Practising once a day is good," states the Silva Method, "practising twice a day is great," and "practising three times a day is excellent." Therefore, begin the process of self-hypnosis by doing it once per day. After some time, progressively increase the number of times you perform it until you are performing it three times each day.

Utilise the well-known autosuggestion that was developed by the French psychologist Emile Coue. This thought process goes something like this: "every day, in every way, I'm getting better and better." In the course of creating those visualisations, be sure to include this idea into your thinking as well.

Using one of the most effective forms of positive affirmation can guarantee that you do, in fact, get better and better as each day passes. As is customary, the goal is to deceive the mind into thinking something other than what is really the case. And of course, you would want things to improve with age, just like wine, right?

- If you want to attain a state of profound relaxation in an efficient manner, you should try using a countdown. You are familiar with the state of calm that we have previously spoken about, right? The one that comes before the most fantastic visualisations and positive affirmations that you will be producing, right? Using a countdown that allows you to count backwards in order to attain that most serene and relaxed state of mind as well as body is the most effective way to achieve this condition, as you will find out when you try it for yourself, is the easiest way to achieve this state.

If you want to follow the Silva Method, you should count backwards from three to one. Be careful to take slow, deep breaths and try to relax as you count down from ten; if you do this, you will be shocked to find that you have entered a trance-like condition by the time you have reached the conclusion of the countdown. If you need more time, you may even count down from 10 to 1 or even 100 to 1 for the greatest possible outcomes. If you do this, you will find that you have additional time.

- Listen to a self-hypnosis chant that has been prerecorded. It may be challenging for some individuals to repeat a self-hypnosis mantra by themselves. If you are one of these people, you may want to think about utilising a self-hypnosis MP3 or perhaps an app in order to make your hypnotic session a lot simpler.

You will discover that there are a great number of free programmes and MP3s that can be downloaded from the internet for usage. On the other hand, if you have any spare cash, you may put it towards some extremely fantastic compensated opportunities. It goes without saying that it is in your best interest to stick to a hypnosis software that was developed by a trained expert that has received accreditation in hypnosis training. In that case, you will discover that it is a great deal less difficult for you to do that hypnosis session on your own.

To get fantastic outcomes, you could try practising fractionation. You should give some thought to participating in the process of fractionation if you want to take that meditation to a whole new level. When you do this, you will discover that you are able to break out of the hypnotic trance, and then, for the greatest possible outcomes, you will be able to go a bit further into the trance. The 'Dolphin Effect' is a term that was coined by Vince Delphin, a well-known personality development coach.

According to this interpretation, awareness is analogous to a dolphin that swims to the surface of the water seeking air before sinking back down to its original depth. Then, after taking another breath of air, it surfaces briefly before resuming its descent into the ocean's depths. Therefore, go into the experience of hypnosis and then further back out, and you will see that each time you move back in, that experience of yours gets deeper. go into the experience of hypnosis and then move farther back out.

- When it comes to your own self-hypnosis, muster all of the intention that you are capable of mustering. Be of the mind that you are determined to make this happen while you are in the process of self-hypnosis. Convince yourself that you are going to alter things for the better via this most marvellous procedure that you are about to start on. You will discover that when you have a strong intention, all of your efforts will not be in vain, and you will actually go a long way towards making that process of hypnosis a success. This is because you will go a long way towards achieving success when you have a solid intention.

If you want to see any sort of good change in your life, you have to believe, all the way down to the most private parts of your being, that it is going to work and help you accomplish all of the things that you want to do. That will guarantee that you make that process of self-hypnosis a magnificent success, and it will also offer you the much-needed confidence that you need in order to traverse that wonderful exercise with the highest degree of élan possible.

In this chapter, we went over everything that needs to be done in order to make sure that we leave no stone unturned when it comes to ensuring that the process of doing self-hypnosis is a resounding success. When it comes to developing a hypnotic session that will certainly kill it, there are, of course, a great number of things that you should not do at all. For that, we need to look at the next and last chapter...

How To Use Neuro-Linguistic Programming (Nlp) To Better Regulate Your Feelings:

Feelings are only alternatives, and there are options available to bring about significant change. When one's sentiments are considered choices rather than experiences that must be suffered through. You are in a position to make choices, and the impact those choices will have on your life is directly proportional to the amount of time and effort you invest in developing these competencies.

As you get more attuned to what you feel, it will become simpler to go back, and you will become aware of the sight or sound that triggered the sensation in the first place. If you install a state of curiosity to discover why you feel that way behind your irritations, frustrations, and fears, then NLP will be able to assist you overcome these negative emotions.

New synapses may be formed with the aid of curiosity. Contributes to the strengthening of the brain and generates a greater level of involvement. When you investigate a solution with a more robust sense of curiosity, you come to the realisation that an incredible number of unfavourable aspects vanish, and you also make room for brand-new opportunities.

If you find that anything irritates you, you should make an effort to prevent your mind from surrounding you with negative ideas. If you do this, you will become stuck in a cycle from which it will be more difficult to break free.

If you make an effort to be more curious, it will stimulate your brain and set you on a whole new path; as a result, you will notice that feelings of annoyance, aggravation, and worry begin to fade away in you. You will start to become aware of how each sensation first manifested itself.

This is the same even if the stimulus is different since the signal contains the emotion. Emotions are created by a signal, and this is the same as well. This occurs in the blink of an eye; the pace is lightning-quick. The only way to do this is to take some deep breaths, calm things down, and carry out the mental task at a leisurely pace.

Before you can recognise the problem-free, flawless being that you are, you need to pause for a second before the cycle restarts so that you can get a clear picture of who you are.

To bring this section to an end, keep in mind the following: locate the track for the feeling in question, eliminate the signal, and instantly replace it with a future in which you face no challenges and are filled with curiosity. If you put in the effort, you will see a significant difference.

The solution to getting rid of depression

There is a strong correlation between auditory signals, or voices in the mind, and negative sentiments. I would like to provide you some advice that will assist you in overcoming your depression.

Depression is quite incapacitating, and it is challenging to find a way to deal with its symptoms. It is essential to reconsider the objective, since sadness makes no sense when an issue or unfortunate event is made to seem personal.

Depression is characterised by a state in which a person does not feel like engaging in any activity, and this state persists to the point that it becomes a habit. It is a difficult way to live; if you feel unhappy, if the world seems to be against you, or if you have the impression that nothing is going to work, you should go within and investigate to see what occurs.

Keep in mind that there is no adversary inside the organisation. If you aren't sure why you're feeling awful, it's a good idea to work under the assumption that there are good reasons behind it.

Perhaps there is a part of you that, despite the fact that you're a fatalist, is trying to help you in some manner. If this is the case, you should assume that these reasons exist.

Pay attention to the voice inside, and if it is a voice that keeps on repeating itself, there are a handful of things you may do: You take a step back, moving away from the picture so that you can see yourself reflected in it. If there's a voice, make it seem like it's coming from the other side of the room.

Make the voice more alluring; it might be the sound of a youngster yawning; maybe it would be best to put it to sleep if you made it seem like a child. The goal is to figure out what mental processes are responsible for the occurrence of an emotion and then to disrupt those mental processes in some way.

You are free to experiment with a variety of submodality shifts until you find anything that provides you with some respite from the heaviness, darkness, or heavy silence that is stored within of you.

Hypnosis

Direct hypnosis and indirect hypnosis are the two varieties of hypnosis that may be practised. When most people hear the word "hypnosis," the image that pops into their heads is of a client or subject sitting with a hypnotherapist. This is an example of direct hypnosis. Using a variety of methods, the hypnotherapist induces hypnosis in the client and helps them through the process. Quite frequently, the customer will seem comfortable when they have their eyes closed. When a person initiates their own hypnotic state, they are said to be practising self-hypnosis.

Hypnosis based on NLP may be beneficial in a single session, but it is significantly more successful when practised repeatedly over a period of time. You have the option of practising NLP hypnosis on your own at home with the use of audio tracks, or you may go to a session in person with a trained NLP hypnotist. This particular kind of hypnosis supports dramatic life changes, including the transformation of your ideas into the physical world.

You may use it to alter your habits or ideas and concentrate on your wants, so getting into the appropriate mentality that will take you there. You can use it to modify your habits or thoughts and focus on your goals. The difference between NLP hypnosis and traditional hypnosis is that the former accesses your subconscious mind, while the latter makes use of suggestive language to lead you in a certain direction while still enabling you to draw your own conclusions. These realisations are ultimately what will influence the course of your life. Your hypnotherapist will have a fair concept of where they want you to go, but they won't be able to tell you precisely what this location will look like in your head unless you describe it to them. For instance, a hypnotherapist could use NLP in order to assist you in quitting smoking; in this case, they are aware that the ultimate objective is to bring you to a point where you have lost the urge to smoke. However, the state of mind you are in and the ideas that you are thinking at this time will define what this location is like, the reasons you are leaving, and any other contributing elements. This is because each person's life is different.

The Process Behind NLP and Hypnosis

The practise of NLP hypnosis is similar to meditation in that it uses the same methods. In order for large and long-lasting changes to occur as a result of NLP hypnosis, the subject has to be willing to embrace the procedure and adhere to the hypnotherapist's verbal direction. The individual will go through substantial and long-lasting changes in proportion to the degree to which they are receptive to the experience. When it comes to getting results, some individuals just need one session, while others have to participate in a significant number of sessions. It does not matter how many sessions there are; the subject has to be actively interested and dedicated to the experience each and every time.

The first step in an NLP hypnosis session is for the person being hypnotised to choose a posture that is both comfortable and allows for total relaxation. In most cases, the subject will be subjected to factors that contribute to their relaxed state being managed in order to guarantee that they stay in that condition for the whole of the session. The temperature is kept at a comfortable level, and any distracting exterior sounds are closely managed. Visual distractions like the light are also muted. White noise or ambient music played in the background is used by certain hypnotherapists. In addition, some hypnotherapists employ aromatherapy by diffusing essential oils in order to help their subjects into a state of deep relaxation. The more laid back the discussion can be on the topic, the more productive the session will be.

After the person being treated has reached their maximum state of relaxation, the NLP therapist will utilise language to assist them into an even deeper state of relaxation. Because of this, the hypnotherapist is able to communicate with the client's subconscious mind. Quite frequently, in order to lead the subject through a visual experience, they will use language that is suggestive and compelling. The linguistic cues that they use stimulate a profound and unconscious shift in the mental processes of the individual. However, in contrast to traditional guided hypnosis, the hypnotherapist does not go into an excessive amount of detail in order to stimulate these ideas. They instead urge the individual to come to these ideas and pictures on their own, which will have an impact that is far more intense, significant, and long-lasting.

Hypnosis based on NLP essentially operates by gaining access to the individual's unconscious thinking processes via the individual's conscious mind. After that, the hypnotherapist is in a position to suggest to the subconscious that it alter its behaviours in order to achieve the desired result. The subconscious provides the foundation for the bulk of our life experiences, including our ideas and emotions, which is one of the reasons why this method is so powerful. The subconscious is where we keep our in-built guide to survival, and it is full with the most fundamental knowledge that influences our assumptions, ideas, and behaviours. Therefore, once we have gained power over our subconscious, we have the ability to modify the core ideas and thoughts that we have.

Utilising Nlp As A Method Of Influence

The primary goal of neuro-linguistic programming, or NLP, is to teach individuals how to get rid of unfavourable feelings, poor habits, mental barriers, internal conflict, and other problems. Another facet of NLP focuses on morally justifiable methods of influencing the opinions of other people, and it's called ethical influence and persuasion. The purpose of this chapter is to provide you with an accurate picture of how hypnosis and persuasion may operate to your benefit by providing an examination of both of these techniques.

The use of hypnosis

The use of certain linguistic patterns to influence another person is a key component of hypnosis. Robert Dilts refers to hypnosis as "sleight of mouth," which is a play on the notion of sleight of hand, which is the capacity of a magician to make objects appear or vanish, even if doing so may seem to be impossible. Milton H. Erickson, a psychiatrist who has done extensive research on the subconscious mind via the use of hypnosis, is considered to be one of the finest hypnotists that has ever been known. Erickson achieved such a high level of mastery in his field that he was able to communicate with the unconscious parts of individuals even when he did not hypnotise them. The term "conversational hypnosis" was coined to describe the method that he used to skillfully hypnotise individuals while they were engaged in mundane, ordinary conversation. He was able to do this anywhere, at any time. In the course of time, hypnosis has evolved into a technique that can not only influence and convince other people, but also assist them in overcoming fear, limiting beliefs, and other obstacles, even while they are not consciously aware of the process. In situations when one is attempting to prevail over opposition, the strategy may be very useful. In the following paragraphs, we will elaborate on hypnosis via discussion.

The hypnotist in a conversational hypnosis session is not a suave somebody who observes you while you enter a hypnotic state. It's possible that Hollywood has influenced you to think that way. In actual practise, hypnosis may take place in the strangest of situations and at the most inopportune of moments. Did you know, for instance, that it is possible to slip into a trance multiple times in a single day? This might happen when you lose track of time, forget why you walked into a room, forget where you put something, or drive to a location and not actually remember going there. It becomes even more intriguing when you consider the fact that even while you are conversing with yourself, strictly speaking, you are in a trance. The only thing that sets apart this kind of hypnosis from conversational hypnosis is the fact that the latter takes place while the subject is engaged in conversation. So, how exactly does it function?

Control Both Consciously and Unconsciously

When a person successfully communicates with their unconscious mind, they enter a trance state. Even when we dream, our bodies are constantly operating in a state of trance, which might be thought of as the "automatic pilot mode." On the other hand, this sort of hypnosis is not quite as terrifying as the realisation that another person can just influence your ideas via their voice. The realisation that your whole life was a procession of hypnotic experiences during which you gained knowledge of the universe and had beliefs ingrained in you ought to provide you with some measure of solace. Because of this, being hypnotised or hypnotising another person may not be such a horrible notion after all so long as you maintain control over your conscious mind.

The true secret that lies underlying conversational hypnosis is the same as the fundamental principle that underlies classical hypnosis. To hypnotise someone during a discussion, all you need to do is block information from entering their conscious brains and urge it to enter their subconscious minds instead. So, can you walk me through that process?

By using certain words and phrases that assist in distracting one's mind: It's interesting to note that some phrases may function almost exactly like keys to the subconscious. Imagine, for example, sends a direct instruction to the subconscious, and the subconscious immediately starts to act on those commands before the conscious mind ever has a chance to filter them. Because this kind of hypnosis relies heavily on visualisation, some phrases have been selected specifically for that purpose. Take an example from the list below.

Timothy is determined to persuade John that expanding their company's reach internationally is the right move for them to make. On the other hand, John does not share this desire, and he explains why by citing a number of valid reasons. Timothy spends a week trying to convince John, but it seems like he is not going to budge from his position. Hypnosis is the next option he will try. Timothy addresses him as follows:

"Imagine if we made this ambition a reality and expanded our operations to other countries. There is a possibility that we may get the attention of some of the other big corporations. Our name will become more well-known, and we will make three times as much money as we do right now, which will lead to a meteoric rise in our earnings. This is our ticket to a happier and more successful existence."

There is a possibility that John has sown the seeds of uncertainty in John's mind, and as a result, John will start to see the opportunities for future achievement in his thoughts. In the end, John will probably give in to the temptation, and forget the reasons that originally pushed him to fire Timothy in the first place. This is a very probable outcome. This is more evidence that the strength of the subconscious mind considerably surpasses that of the conscious mind by a significant margin.

By using obfuscation and ambiguity in their statements: It is not uncommon to hear inhabitants of various nations grumbling that their country continue to elect the same incompetent leaders at every election. Now, given the degree of literacy of many people around the globe, you would assume that we as a race are more likely to be inclined to make judgements that are more sensible. But that is not the case. This makes perfect logic, but what you fail to realise is that most politicians throughout the globe intentionally leave a lot of room for interpretation and use ambiguous language. In point of fact, all these individuals are is a collection of accomplished public speakers. Maintain vigilance the next time there is a political campaign in your neighbourhood so you may demonstrate that this assertion is correct. Take attention of the language, and more precisely, the phrases, that these politicians employ in order to win the compassion of citizens and earn votes. You will come to the realisation that their speeches often lack logic and are full of vague phrases and are ambiguous, having no real aims other than to toy with the emotions of the audience. You will come to this realisation because you will come to realise that their speeches are ambiguous. If a leader wants to employ communication that is straightforward and without ambiguity, they have a decreased chance of winning since they are less likely to be able to stir up the passions of the audience.

It's possible that you're confused about how language that's both imprecise and ambiguous works. It is not complicated;

If someone speaks to you in a logical sequence or tells you sentences that make sense, your mind will get to work and begin to decode what the speaker is saying. If someone talks to you in a logical sequence or tells you phrases that make no sense, your mind will not go to work. In the event that you accomplish this, your mind will likewise be searching for openings in the code as it is attempting to decode it. If, on the other hand, I make use of ambiguous phrases and words, there is a possibility that it will have a significant impact on the thought processes of a large number of people. While the voter is still attempting to decipher what the speaker is saying, the speaker is already barraging them with information that is more nebulous, which will overcome the voter's desire to make rational judgements and merely get them to vote for them.

For instance, a politician may address the populace of a certain city, urging them to rise to the occasion and welcome the impending shift in order to achieve their goals. In addition to this, he would reassure them that the opportunity is there and that they are capable of seizing it.

When a politician keeps hammering people with the idea that they should vote for him, there is a chance that some voters in the throng may start to ask what problem is being solved, what kind of change is required, and what time it is. Before it receives any information received from the conscious mind, the suggestion is first processed by the subconscious mind.

Then, Exactly, Can You Explain What Neuro-Linguistic Programming Is?

In its most fundamental form, it may be seen as a method or a collection of guidelines for attaining self-improvement, adjusting behaviour, and establishing more successful interpersonal interactions. It is often analogous to self-hypnosis and takes into consideration certain presumptions about the ways in which language influences the neurofunctional processes of the brain. The foundation of this argument is that in order to be successful, to conquer your worries, and to build your self-confidence, you must see your objectives in great detail and model suitable patterns of behaviour. Its name comes from the way in which our senses digest events before storing them away in our brains (which are called neurons). Then there is the way in which we employ language or symbols to form mental images (linguistic). Last but not least, the process through which desirable routines and behaviours eventually become imprinted in our life (programming).

The primary goal of neurolinguistic programming (NLP) is to first identify and then modify ingrained habits of thinking and behaviour. Once you have a solid grasp of each individual component of the picture, the strategies become rather easy to execute. On the other hand, as you continue to practise the NLP procedures, you could discover that your grasp of all that is possible to achieve deepens and becomes more nuanced. Imagine that you are modelling yourself after a good salesman. In the beginning, you should begin by asking the salesman questions, paying attention to what they do, and listening to all that they say. The next thing you pick up on is the intonation and tone of their voice while they are on the phone, or how they imitate the words of another person to have a better grasp of the requirements or wishes of that person. You watch their body language as well as the expressions on their faces. Soon enough, you begin to copy the salesman in your own profession by emulating the tone of their voice, their body language, and other aspects of their demeanour. This provides you with all of the skills essential to become successful by obtaining self-improvement, adjusting your behaviour, and acquiring more effective interpersonal interactions. You are using NLP at the workplace as well as in your personal life.

According to the Psychology Dictionary, NLP is "a collection of strategies which were devised to improve the interpersonal relationships and levels of communication between individuals by evaluating and modifying current mental models of the world which individuals develop and use to respond to, and interact with, the environment and other people." NLP was developed to improve interpersonal relationships and levels of communication between individuals by evaluating and modifying current mental models of the world which individuals develop and use to respond to, and interact with, the environment and other people. 2

It is not difficult to find someone who has not employed NLP at some point in their life; in many cases, they have done so without even being aware of it. Let's imagine you get the impression that someone does not like you or that they have spoken negatively about you behind your back. You fortify your defences very instantly, and it quickly becomes obvious to you that the other person does not like you. You have simply persuaded yourself that it is true, regardless of whether or not it really is. How about being an expert in a certain set of skills? You may either go into it with the mindset that there is little likelihood that you will ever become excellent at this particular ability, or you can choose to ignore this mindset and keep working hard until you achieve success. Your frame of mind will determine the nature of the results. What if, rather of responding to an unpleasant statement, you tried to find the good in that person? Perhaps that person is having a horrible day or just found out about some tragedy, and they are merely passing their anger or fear to you. What if you tried to see the good in that person? Yes, along with that set of skills you are certain you will never be able to fully master. What happens if you trick yourself into thinking that you already have it mastered, and then you force yourself to keep doing it until you do? You will be successful in all aspects of your life if you have a positive attitude towards everything that happens in it.

You can't learn NLP by reading about it or thinking about it before you really know it. It is something that you carry out on a consistent basis. What are some of the benefits of engaging in NLP training? in order to feel better. Practise is absolutely necessary if you want to achieve mastery in the vast majority of endeavours. If you practise NLP, you will become a better communicator, you will be able to achieve your objectives, and you will enhance not just your present circumstance but also all other aspects of your life. However, it is your responsibility to make the decision, and making choices involves both purpose and expertise. If you have the intention to make a change in your life, it indicates that you are prepared to put up the necessary work. Competence is the instrument you use to make things happen. However, there is not an NLP course manual available that is tailored to the exact needs of each and every individual. Learning NLP offers you the capacity to recognise thinking and behaviour patterns and either duplicate them or disrupt them completely. If you have gained and knowledge of NLP, and put that understanding into practise, then it indicates that you have removed the training wheels, and you are well on your way to comprehending the larger picture of what NLP is.

Breaks In The Loop And Interrupts In The Pattern

Within the human body, the brain is without a doubt the organ that has the greatest degree of complexity. Even during ordinary activities such as directing the different parts of the body for movement in elementary motor skills all the way up to making critical and complicated judgements in real time, it is necessary to conduct an astounding amount of computations per second. This is because even the simplest motor skills need this. The brain is one of the most powerful pieces of biological gear that humans possess since it is responsible for making millions of these interrelated choices on a daily basis.

However, we do not yet have a complete understanding of the breadth of its intricacy and the inner workings of the system. We do know one thing, and that is that the human brain is exclusively responsible for allowing individuals to cultivate thought patterns and habits, which ultimately control not just people's day-to-day behaviours but also their thought patterns. It does this in an effort to maximise the day-to-day actions and mental processes of a person, but the results of taking these shortcuts aren't always to the individual's advantage.

In order for the brain to create these "loops" or "patterns," it goes through a series of procedures that not only assist it in developing a particular habit but also assist it in incorporating that habit into everyday life. When it comes to natural language programming (NLP), having a firm grasp of the idea of cognition in its broadest sense is very necessary. In the following section, we will begin by taking a cursory look at this concept. Simply put, cognition is the study of how the brain takes in information and formulates mental representations of that data in a person's head. It explains how the brain works and helps us put that knowledge to use in practical applications.

Neuropsychology is the name of the field of research that focuses on determining whether or not there is a connection between learning and cognition. This is an area of research that I used to specialise in myself. Many psychologists have been studying the nuances of neurology for some decades now, and this field has fascinated scientists for as long as the notion has been around. Each of these individuals produced ideas that detailed how the human brain operates and how it learns, beginning with Pavlov and John Watson's description of classical conditioning all the way up to B. F. Skinner's description of operant conditioning.

It is common knowledge that a person's day-to-day routines and the patterns of thought they engage in will, in the end, determine how productive and successful they are. Despite the fact that habits are not biassed, they will either assist a person in achieving their goals or in being consistent in their pursuit of those goals. Or, alternatively, they will take measures to guarantee that they maintain the same average or terrible outcomes that they have always obtained. According to what Dr. Bandler had to say about the matter, "Brains aren't designed to get results; they just go in directions."

In terms of general behaviour, it is typically simply a matter of knowing your ABCs, so to speak, which means learning the sequence of the antecedent, behaviour, and consequence. In other words, memorising the ABCs is the key to understanding general behaviour. This idea was first derived from B. F. Skinner's model of habit formation, which states that cognition, antecedent, behaviour, and consequence are the three primary phases involved in the process of becoming a habit. The following is a condensed explanation of what they are:

Ancillary Factors

The stimuli that come before a behaviour or response are known as its antecedents. It is conditions and circumstances that a person finds themselves in that lead them to act in a certain way. The results of a certainbehaviour are determined by the antecedents that automatically bring about that behaviour.

To put it another way, antecedents are the individuals and circumstances that prompt a certain response or behaviour. They are the foundation upon which habits are built, and they are the primary determinant of how a person responds to any given circumstance.

The antecedents are investigated in order to determine, on the whole, whether the response is due to the application of positive reinforcement or negative punishment. When one has such information, it is much simpler to forecast future behaviour. The manipulation of antecedents in order to provoke the behaviour that is intended is not too difficult to do.

Acquiring Confidence Through The Use Of Nlp

It is essential to have self-assurance in order to succeed in today's culture, which places a premium on those who are driven, ambitious, and charismatic. However, although it may come naturally to some people, others may find that possessing and expressing confidence is a challenge that has to be addressed. Even while being successful and having the power to influence people is both wonderful and beneficial, we still need confidence in order to do these things. Fortunately, NLP presents us with a variety of strategies that may be used to boost our confidence. Anchoring is a strategy that is both successful and straightforward, which is why it is recommended so highly by such a large number of NLP practitioners and users. Although there are a few distinct ways to NLP, we would want to concentrate on one in particular. In the context of neuro-linguistic programming (NLP), an anchor is anything that facilitates our transition into a desirable mental state or frame of mind. If we want to look confident, for example, at a crucial job interview, we would remember a past instance in which we were actually confident. This would help us appear more certain. We would do it again and allow it to serve as a reminder of our entire potential. Putting it another way, doing so connects the confident sentiments we had in the past with the situation in the here and now in which we wish to have the same confident sensations. These are several sources that often provide strong anchors:

Sounds Aromas and Gastronomy Songs

In point of fact, you most likely already own your very own anchors without ever being aware of them. Every one of us has had the experience when we listened to an old song, and it brought back memories of a certain summer when we went to the beach. Or, maybe we caught a whiff of a fragrance or perfume that brought back memories of a certain individual. In reality, we encounter anchors rather often during the course of our lives. On the other hand, when you study NLP, you will learn how to consciously establish your own anchors, which you can then use for a variety of objectives.

Establishing a firm foundation for self-assurance

There are a number of efficient methods that can be used to make and effectively employ anchors, but we strongly recommend you to take the procedures that are outlined below in order to establish an anchor that may assist you in gaining or increasing your level of confidence. How to do it:

The first thing you need to do is think of a time when you felt the most confident version of yourself (or, if you truly can't think of one, try to envisage a time when you would feel the most confident version of yourself).

The second step of this exercise is to think about any modalities (sights, sounds, scents, tastes, and bodily emotions) that you recall experiencing during the moment of confidence that you choose or the moment that you imagined; doing so will make this exercise more powerful and successful. The goal here is to conjure up an impression that is as powerful as is humanly feasible with as many details as you can. Take note of how you are feeling and focus your attention on that sensation as you continue to do this. Do you have a sense of dominance? Who can stop them? Are you satisfied? Do you believe that you have the ability to triumph over each challenge that you face?

Step 3: While you are working to strengthen your memory of confidence, grab the thumb and pointer finger of one hand and squeeze the thumbnail of the other hand. Do this while continuing to establish your strongest memory.

Step 4 is to take it easy. Engage in a new activity to create some space in your head.

Test your anchor as the fifth step. Make a pinch with the same fingers on the same thumbnail. If you've done a good job of establishing an anchor, performing something like this should bring to memory a strong and self-assured experience that you've either previously remembered or produced. If this doesn't work, there's no need to worry about it. Begin with the first stage. Because it needs your undivided attention and effort throughout the process, developing a successful anchor may require more than one attempt.

Squeeze your thumb and let the anchoring moment to take over whenever you find yourself in need of accessing a confident mentality or just needing a confidence boost (because let's face it, we all need one at some time). Your perspective should shift into one that is more confident as a result of this, which will serve you well in whatever endeavour you do.

Psychopaths Are Incapable Of Feeling The Suffering Of Other People In Any Way.

Psychopaths are emotionally cold-hearted. Because of this, they don't need to physically touch their victims in order to inflict terrible harm on others around them. They use other people as a source of entertainment and profit, and they do it without giving any thought to how they would feel if the same treatment were meted out to them. They give the impression of emotional detachment and are profoundly narcissistic, which means that they are only concerned with whatever is going on in their own heads, and as a result, they are unable to feel empathy for other people. In addition to this, they exhibit the barest minimum of anxiety. However, they are content to see these feelings in other people, whether it be extreme happiness or anger, since it gives them the opportunity to express these feelings themselves. And sociopaths take pleasure in upsetting the emotional state of other people because, in their minds, it serves as a means of expression and provides a stage upon which they may exercise their creative ability to manipulate others and deceive themselves. Because your emotions are the most powerful weapon a psychopath can use against you, it is important to be mindful of how you respond when one approaches you with the intention of manipulating them.

Psychopaths have a superior attitude and a sense of entitlement.

Psychopaths, like narcissistic people, believe that they deserve every single thing that they need, and as a result, they are highly likely to behave in an entitled manner. They often make their demands without being courteous enough, and when they are denied, rather than searching for a better way to ask, they frequently resort to manipulating others and engaging in blackmail as a means of obtaining what they need. They do this rather than looking for better ways to ask. Even though they haven't put in much effort to get things, psychopaths often believe that they are entitled to everything. As a result, rather than joining the competition or waiting in line as regular people do to get what they want, psychopaths frequently resort to using shortcuts or going around the proper channels to achieve their goals. Then, when they are prevented from moving forward, they don't mind causing a disruption. Another feature of their arrogance is that they have a condescending attitude towards other people and believe that they are deserving of competing with only the very best, despite the fact that it is possible that they do not have the skill for that or that they have not put in sufficient effort to merit being placed in such a high cadre. They quickly find themselves embroiled in an egotistical fight, and when they see there is nothing they can do to achieve the 'breakthrough' that they so desperately want, they have no choice but to pack it in and move on. It is possible that their egocentric behaviour is the reason why they are unable to remain at a single workplace for an extended period of time. Their ingrained sense of superiority will inevitably lead them to behave in a manner that is inconsistent with the way things really are. When they don't succeed in ascending up that radar as fast as they intended to, they often are unable to handle the internal humiliation that comes along with it. Because of this, they have a tendency to often up and leave.

Psychopaths are of the opinion that the rules should be followed by everyone. But psychopaths, being the narcissists that they are, often find it difficult to adhere to the rules and regulations that have been enacted by the leadership of a body or an organisation. This is because psychopaths see themselves as above such constraints. Because of this, they are likely to be disruptive students at their schools and uncooperative employees who refuse to work together with their coworkers. They never fully get over the rebellion of their ancestors, and as a result, the majority of the time, they are citizens who do not obey the law and are capable of committing crimes. They have a pattern of disobeying the rules and will often engage in illegal activity for no other reason than the fact that they like it or the rush of adrenaline that it provides. This provided them with the illusion of invincibility or supremacy over the rest of the population, as if they were flying over the heads of everyone else and were unable to be caught. They also have a propensity to repeatedly break the rule because their feeling of "seeking their edge of adventure" is so strong that it is impossible to restrain them from doing so.

The Use Of Nlp In Business

The use of Chunking and Meta-Programs

Meta programmes and chunking both have the potential to be quite useful in professional contexts. They are basically filters that affect how you interpret the world around you and have a big effect on how you behave and how you interact with others. They also define how you view the world around you. When striving to comprehend another person's perceptions of the world, including his beliefs, limiting beliefs, and choices, the Meta Model is a useful and helpful tool (Corballis, 2012).

You can chunk up in NLP, or you can chunk down. Both methods are valid.

When you break things down into smaller chunks, you can see the greater picture. queries such as "What is this a part of?" are good examples of chunking up queries. The question, "What's the bottom line?" "What is the intention behind all of this?"

The act of taking something and analysing it from a more in-depth or particular point of view is referred to as "chunking down." The following are some examples of questions that may be used to chunk down a scenario: "If I were to cut this situation into slices, what would it look like?" and "What are the specifics of this situation?" "Are you able to provide me with an illustration?"

When doing business and for the sake of negotiation, it is beneficial to either chunk up or chunk down until you and the other party are able to reach an agreement on the matter. Because of this approach, you and the other person may come to an understanding with one another and bring new perspectives into play to bring them up to the same level.

Meta-Programs and Chunking need regular practise, just like everything else in this book, but they have the potential to be extremely useful once they are learned.

The Quickening of Instruction

Learning occurs outside of the confines of the traditional classroom setting. Even after they have received their degrees, workers continue to be deluged with a great deal of material that they are required to read through. Products and emerging technologies level the playing ground, which is especially important in markets that are already competitive. These innovative developments have the potential to change your performance as an employee as well as a corporation. Utilisingpractises designed for fast learning will make it much simpler for you to pick up new skills.

Using essential ideas that are connected to NLP, accelerated learning procedures further maximise the capacity of the brain to accept, process, and retain knowledge in an extremely short amount of time.

There are several advantages that come along with incorporating accelerated learning into your company. When compared to more traditional methods of training for new workers, accelerated training courses cut both the amount of time and money spent on training. Because accelerated learning courses are designed with the student as the primary focus, this method of imparting knowledge is much more efficient.

In addition to enhancing the capabilities of new workers, rapid learning may also be enhanced in the workplace, particularly when employees are attending meetings. When businesspeople get together, they often talk about serious topics and share a lot of knowledge.

When workers are presented with an overwhelming amount of material, they often get disengaged from the conversation, which results in ineffective meetings. Through the use of accelerated learning methodologies, large amounts of knowledge are efficiently broken down into more manageable chunks for the workers. In addition, the adoption of these strategies helps to pique the attention of participants, which in turn makes activities more engaging.

NLP: Reprogram Your Mind to Eliminate Stress, Anxiety, Fear, and Depression is the Topic of Chapter 7 of the Book.

It is necessary for one to have an understanding of these principles before moving further with the process of programming the mind to get rid of stress, worry, fear, and sadness.

• Stress is the body's response to specific changes that demand a person to adapt to them or respond to them in some way. The body may respond to these changes either physically, cognitively, or in any combination of the two.

• Anxiety is a mental state that is characterised by a sensation of concern, and it may be caused by a number of different things.

• Fear is an emotional response that is created when an individual perceives that they are in danger, will be harmed, or will experience pain.

• Depression is a mental condition that is characterised by changes in mood as well as a lack of interest in day-to-day activities.

Stress, anxiety, fear, and depression all have some characteristics in common.

These mental states have some similarities, and those similarities include the following:

- Heartburn and indigestion

The mental state described above may be responsible for a decrease in the amount of blood and oxygen that flow to the stomach. Inflammation, an imbalance in the stomach, or a disruption in blood flow might result from this. In the end, this results in indigestion since it has an effect on digestion.

- A diminished ability to consume food

These states of mind have an effect on a person's hunger and appetite. They have an effect on the digestive system as well as the stomach, which might cause an individual to lose their appetite.

- An irregular and rapid heartbeat

The depicted mental state causes an increase in the rate and frequency of palpitations in the heart as a response to the circumstances. This helps to maintain a balance between the high quantities of oxygen that are wasted at these periods by organs in the body such as the mind and the stomach.

- Difficulties falling asleep or staying asleep

The aforementioned mental states have one thing in common: they all influence a person's ability to sleep. When a person is sleep deprived, their normal sleeping habits are disrupted. Insomnia is the term used to describe this condition.

- Hands that are icy and wet with perspiration

The medical term for this condition is hyperhidrosis. It is a condition in which there is an abnormally high level of activity in the sympathetic nervous system. The arteries get constricted, which in turn causes an over stimulation of the glands that are responsible for sweating. Because of this occurrence, blood flow to the hands is restricted, which causes the hands to become clammy and chilly.

· a putting on of weight

When under stress, the body has a mechanism that works to maintain hormonal checks and balances, which may have an effect on how much weight you acquire. Because of this, when these emotional states are not regulated properly, it might result in bad eating habits. A rise in cholesterol level may be the result of poor eating habits, which may also contribute to an increase in body weight. This phenomenon may also make it difficult for the body to shed extra pounds when it does not need to.

• Difficulties in the sexual arena

These emotional states have an effect on a person's capacity to provide sexual satisfaction to their partner. When men are in these emotional states, they are more likely to suffer from erectile dysfunction.

The Unbounded Potential That Exists Within Each Of Us

The human intellect has the highest potential of any kind of intelligence in the whole universe. If you put in the effort and direct your attention to the appropriate areas, there is no ceiling on what you can do with your mind. This indicates that any ordinary person, such as a farmer named Joe, is capable of solving a mathematical problem authored by Albert Einstein if they have the correct mindset, approach, and practise. To some people, this may seem like a tremendous phenomena, but to others, it may sound like I'm just making creative use of words. The fact that this is not true is quite astonishing. It is the truth or the reality with which we are tasked with grappling and coming to terms. The question is, what does this mean for both of us?

What it implies is that if you approach a subject in the right way, your mind may be able to assist you solve problems that cannot be solved by current science. It implies that with the right technique, we can transform a dream or an idea that was conceived in our minds into a historical accomplishment that will change the course of our lives. It indicates that with the correct skills, we may live the lives of our dreams and accomplish the objectives we have set for ourselves to last a lifetime. This may also come out as a quite incredible assertion. Permit me to inquire anything of you. Did you know that the tablet or gadget you are using to read this book was once just a collection of thoughts in someone's head? You obviously do; you just haven't considered it in that light before! Did you know that you can teach your mind to guide you in the right direction, which is the road that leads to success?

Before we continue, I feel obligated to remind you that elevating your life to new heights via the power of your mind is not a simple task. Because playing with someone's mind in the wrong manner is never a smart idea, this is difficult task that will need devotion and a method that has been proved effective. On the other hand, notwithstanding the nature of your hopes and aspirations, it is quite possible to realise them and even surpass them. How? You may try using NLP, which stands for "neuro-linguistic programming." This is a relatively recent scientific theory that enables people to retrain their minds to a certain degree. Throughout the many years that I have spent studying NLP, I have come to the conclusion that the primary barrier that prevents most individuals from reaching their goals is a life filled with regularity and habit. The Neuro-Linguistic Programming (NLP) methodology compels you to retrain your brain and break free from the shackles of habit and routine. You may pull yourself out of any habit or rut you're in by altering the way you think in your mind. This will allow you to realise who you really are, which will impact not just your life but also the lives of people around you. I will demonstrate how you may use NLP to accomplish particular objectives, such as getting rid of phobias, in order to assist you get a better understanding of NLP.

Techniques Of Effective Reframing Based On Nlp

NLP stands for neurolinguistic programming. It may be argued that frames are one of the most essential concepts, if not the most important idea, in the body of knowledge that is referred to as NLP. "The map is not the territory" is an age-old proverb that is drilled into every NLP practitioner's head. This indicates that our interpretation of reality is not the same thing as reality itself.

Everything that we go through in life is subjective, which means that there are always connotations associated with it that people aren't consciously aware of. People live as if the matrix is real and buy into it, not realising that what they are seeing is reality filtered through their own perceptions and frames of reference. To put it another way, frames are what give an occurrence or event in life its meaning and place in its context. To be able to recognise something and go outside of its confines in order to see it for what it is is already a powerful experience. The grip on fake reality is loosened as a result.

In the absence of frames, human beings will only ever exist in the present and experience life in the same way that animals do, with no preconceived notions of the past or the future, connections, or the significance of things. Everything becomes into an isolated occurrence that is disconnected from everything else. Existence requires the presence of frameworks. And those who are aware of how to actively exert control over it are in a position to influence the reality that others take to be the case!

He Whoever has control over the frame also has control over the game.

Let us assume for the moment that we do not have any influence on the sequence of events that occurs in a certain situation. Despite the fact that we have very little to no control over the event itself, we can still influence how it feels to be there. For the meaning to shift would need a shift in reality itself. The very fabric of how reality is experienced!

You are able to reframe every aspect of an individual's experience and mental structure, including his views, identity or self-concept, personal value, actions, capabilities, and so on. This is true whether you are talking about an individual's beliefs, identity, or self-concept.

It is helpful to describe the challenge for reframing work as X eual Y (complex equivalency) or X caue Y (Cause and Effect) for the sake of simplicity. Although it is possible to construct an endless number of custom frames (for the established NLP pattern, please see the Mindline or Sleight of Mouth Pattern), there are an infinite number of frames that may be designed.

Let's say that the problematic statement is "I am stupid(x), and that's the reason I can't get promoted(y)" You may examine it from a Cause and Effect or Complex Equivalence perspective, and then reframe it in accordance with that perspective.

My incompetence is the root cause of my inability to advance in my career.

The fact that I'm not being promoted has something to do with how dumb I am.

Now that we have a clear understanding of the issue, we can begin to work on changing the meaning. You are free to make adjustments to either X or Y, or even both!

Let's play a (dumb) word game: The reason I can't be promoted is because I have too many responsibilities already!

Since I am not really suited for my occupation, it is impossible for me to advance in my career.

Let's go have some fun with Y (who can't move up):

I've hit rock bottom, which is why I've decided to stick it out in this pointless work. I'm stuck, which is why I'm not maximising my true potential and looking for a position where my talents can be used (y). I'm looking for a job where my talents can be utilised.

In practise, we do not want to use any negative identity descriptors such as "my stupidity," thus in order to reframe both that and the outcome, we would have to remove any negative identity descriptors.

Due to the fact that I am both overqualified and underutilized(x), my current position is not a good use of my abilities, and as a result, I am unable to advance in my career(y).

The recasting of uahe any that was done above negativity and self-esteem have been flipped on the subject, so that he should now feel more empowered or have more confidence as a result of the simple act of switching the Xs and the Ys.

In addition to this, you may even reframe the world itself without affecting the X and Y coordinates in any way.

Putting that unsecure worker in an environment where there is both a recession and no job opportunities to be had? Will it immediately transform into something else?

"The only reason I can't move up in the company is because I'm an idiot." -- in a world where seventy percent of the people is unemployed.

www.ingramcontent.com/pod-product-compliance
Lightning Source LLC
Chambersburg PA
CBHW050418120526
44590CB00015B/2012